Revising the
Constitution

Margaret King

Publishing Credits

Rachelle Cracchiolo, M.S.Ed., *Publisher*
Conni Medina, M.A.Ed., *Managing Editor*
Nika Fabienke, Ed.D., *Series Developer*
June Kikuchi, *Content Director*
Seth Rogers, *Editor*
Michelle Jovin, M.A., *Assistant Editor*
Kevin Pham, *Graphic Designer*

TIME For Kids and the TIME For Kids logo are registered trademarks of TIME Inc. Used under license.

Image Credits: Cover and p.1 United States Capitol; p.5 Constitutional Convention (w/c on paper), Ferris, Jean Leon Gerome (1863-1930)/Private Collection/Bridgeman Images; pp.6, 12–13, 31 North Wind Picture Archives; p.8 Joseph Siffred Duplessis (1725-1802), Oil on canvas, circa 1785 National Portrait Gallery, Smithsonian Institution, Gift of The Morris and Gwendolyn Cafritz Foundation, NPG.87.43; pp.8–9 Ian Dagnall/ Alamy Stock Photo; p.11 (inset) Fine Art Images Heritage Images/Newscom; p.15 (top left) National Archives [1667751], (top right) National Archives [1408042], (bottom) The White House Historical Association; p.18 Gift of Edgar William and Bernice Chrysler Garbisch, 1963, Metropolitan Museum of Art, Accession Number 63.201.2; p.24 National Gallery of Art; p.25 United States Capitol; p.28 Tomas Abad/Alamy Stock Photo; p.29 Robert W. Kelley/The LIFE Picture Collection/Getty Images; pp.32–33 The Battle of Lexington, 19th April 1775, 1910 (oil on canvas), Wollen, William Barnes (1857-1936)/National Army Museum, London/Bridgeman Images; p.33 Copyright Museums Victoria/CC BY (Licensed as Attribution 4.0 International); p.35 Rue des Archives/ Granger, NYC; pp.36–37 Jan Walters/Alamy Stock Photo; p.38 Richard Levine/Alamy Stock Photo; p.39 Buyenlarge/Getty Images; pp.40–41 Michael Ventura/Alamy Stock/ National Archives[12167793]; all other images from iStock and/or Shutterstock.

Library of Congress Cataloging-in-Publication Data

Names: King, Margaret (Margaret Esther), author.
Title: Just right words : revising the constitution / Margaret King.
Description: Huntington Beach, CA : Teacher Created Materials, 2017. | Includes index.
Identifiers: LCCN 2017023529 (print) | LCCN 2017023697 (ebook) | ISBN 9781425854683 (eBook) | ISBN 9781425849924 (pbk.)
Subjects: LCSH: Constitutional history--United States--Juvenile literature. | United States. Constitution--Juvenile literature. | United States--Politics and government--1783-1789--Juvenile literature.
Classification: LCC KF4541 (ebook) | LCC KF4541 .K56 2017 (print) | DDC 342.7302/92--dc23
LC record available at https://lccn.loc.gov/2017023529

Teacher Created Materials

5301 Oceanus Drive
Huntington Beach, CA 92649-1030
http://www.tcmpub.com

ISBN 978-1-4258-4992-4
© 2018 Teacher Created Materials, Inc.
Made in China
Nordica.092017.CA21701119

Table of Contents

Law of the Land

When you play a sport, you follow a set of rules. Did you know there is also a set of rules for how to run the United States government? The U.S. Constitution is the highest law in the nation. It has rules for **electing** leaders and making laws. It also spells out the rights each person has.

The men who wrote the Constitution in 1787 described a government that could adapt, yet **endure**. The document they crafted has been **amended** many times. It is still guiding the nation after more than 230 years.

Fixed or Flexible?

Over the years, scholars have argued about how to **interpret** the Constitution. Should the country stick to the exact words of the document's writers, or is it better to interpret those words to fit the times? Lawmakers have been arguing over this topic since the Constitution was written. Even the Founding Fathers couldn't agree.

THINK LINK

❯ Why does a country need a constitution?

❯ What would happen if one leader had all of the power?

❯ Should the U.S. Constitution be updated, or should it stay the same? Why?

Becoming a Nation

In 1783, the American colonies won a war to end British rule. The 13 colonies became 13 free states. Leaders signed the Articles of Confederation, which allowed the states to elect a **congress**. But this congress did not have the power to collect taxes or raise an army. Instead, each state had its own money and **militia**. The states had no way to join together.

General George Washington had led the states in the war for independence. He warned that the nation would have a hard road ahead. He believed the states must **unite**.

Farmers Fight Back

After the war, some people borrowed money from the government to start farms. But farming was expensive, and many people could not pay their debts. Those people were thrown in jail. In 1786, Daniel Shays led a revolt of farmers in Massachusetts. Shays and his followers were defeated. But Shays's Rebellion made many people think there should be a stronger government.

ARTICLES
OF
CONFEDERATION
AND
PERPETUAL UNION
BETWEEN THE
STATES
OF
HAMPSHIRE, MASSACHUSETTS-BAY, RHODE-ISLAND
AND PROVIDENCE PLANTATIONS, CONNECTICUT, NEW-
YORK, NEW-JERSEY, PENNSYLVANIA, DELAWARE, MARY-
LAND, VIRGINIA, NORTH-CAROLINA, SOUTH-CAROLINA
AND GEORGIA.

LANCASTER, (PENNSYLVANIA,) PRINTED:
BOSTON, RE-PRINTED BY JOHN GILL,
PRINTER TO THE GENERAL ASSEMBLY.
M,DCC,LXXVII.

Spirit of 1776

Colonial leaders signed the Declaration of Independence in 1776. It said the colonies were free states. But it did not say they were a nation. Benjamin Franklin was one of the leaders who signed the document. He called for unity. "We must all hang together, or **assuredly** we shall all hang separately," he said.

Calling All States

James Madison and Alexander Hamilton also thought the states must join together. In 1786, they led the call for a **convention**. It would be held the following summer. They asked states to send **delegates** to meet in Philadelphia. Heavy rains in the spring had left roads muddy. It took weeks for all of the delegates to get there.

The session, or meeting, opened at last on May 25, 1787. The delegates all had great respect for Washington, so they chose him to lead the sessions. Madison served as secretary. He took notes on each day of the debate.

Meet the Delegates

The delegates at the convention were all white men. Most of them were wealthy. Rhode Island did not send anyone, but the other 12 states picked 74 delegates. Only 55 men showed up in Philadelphia. Franklin, at 81 years old, was the oldest. John Dayton of New Jersey was the youngest at 26 years old.

Secret Sessions

The delegates wanted to feel free to speak their minds without the fear of judgment, so they kept their debates completely secret from the public. Guards stood outside the meeting room. The door was locked and the windows were nailed shut. Delegates sweat in the stuffy room as they argued through a long, hot summer.

The Great Compromise

The delegates debated for weeks. Washington, Madison, and Hamilton argued for a strong **federal** government. Other delegates wanted to protect the rights of states. Those from small states were afraid that big states would grab all the power. It seemed like the delegates would never agree on a new government.

Finally, they found ways to **compromise**. To protect the rights of both big and small states, delegates agreed on a congress with two groups. These two groups would be known as the *houses of congress*. One house would be elected based on population. In the other house, all states would be equal. This agreement was known as the *Great Compromise*.

A New Start

When the delegates first met, their plan was to make the Articles of Confederation stronger. But they soon changed their goal. They began to create a whole new government. The meeting became known as the Constitutional Convention. The delegates were later called the **Framers** of the Constitution.

Houses of Congress

The House of Representatives		The Senate
435	Number of Members	100
2 Years	Length of Terms	6 Years
25	Minimum Age to Serve	30
By Population	Representation of the States	Equal

No More Kings

The United States had fought a war to be free of the British king. To lead the new government, delegates decided on an elected president. Hamilton wanted the president to serve for life. Others thought that sounded a lot like a king. They agreed the president's term should be four years.

Split Over Slavery

There was one major problem with the Great Compromise. Delegates could not agree on how enslaved people would be counted. Northern states had more free people. Southern states had more enslaved people. As it stood, northern states would have more **representatives** in congress.

Unspoken Evil

Some delegates hoped to end slavery. But many Southerners counted on enslaved people to work on their **plantations**. Constitution writers kept the words *slave* and *slavery* out. Instead, the writers used the term *other persons*. And they did not write that slavery should be stopped.

Delegates from southern states wanted to count enslaved people in their populations. Northern delegates said that was not fair. Gouverneur Morris, a delegate from Pennsylvania, said, "Are they men? Then make them citizens and let them vote." In the end, delegates reached a disturbing deal. They would count each enslaved person as three-fifths of a person—not as a citizen.

enslaved people picking cotton

Keep Talking

The rules of the convention let delegates change their minds. Even after they voted on an issue, someone could raise it again. This meant delegates could move forward without getting stuck on one issue. They kept talking until they found a way to compromise.

We the People

The delegates agreed on a new government with three branches—legislative, executive, and judicial. The branches would be separate. But they would have checks and balances, so no branch could grow too strong.

Delegates chose Morris to write the final document. The Constitution opens with a section called the **Preamble**. A draft of the Preamble began, "We the people of the states of New Hampshire, Massachusetts," and so on. It listed all of the states. Morris changed it to, "We the People of the United States." This was the first time the country had been called "the United States." The states were now speaking as one nation.

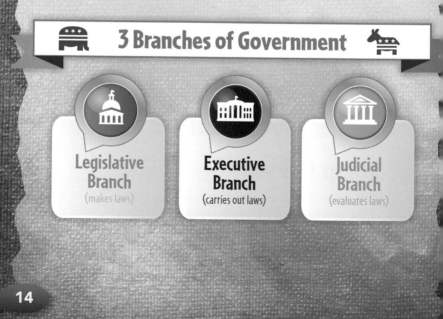

3 Branches of Government

Legislative Branch (makes laws)

Executive Branch (carries out laws)

Judicial Branch (evaluates laws)

Short and to the Point

The U.S. Constitution says a lot without using a lot of words. As written by the Framers, it had around 4,400 words. That makes it the shortest written constitution in the world. It is also the oldest one that is still in use.

Founding Father

James Madison was a small man. One friend said he was "no bigger than half a piece of soap." But he had a huge role in creating the Constitution, from guiding the debate to pushing to get the document **ratified**. That is why Madison is called the Father of the Constitution.

Making the Laws

The Constitution has seven articles, or parts. Article I is about the legislative branch, or Congress. Its job is to make laws. Congress has two houses. One is called the House of Representatives. People in each state elect members based on how many people live in their states. The other house is called the Senate. People of each state elect two members to the Senate.

Congress passes laws to carry out the powers of the federal government. These include the power to collect taxes, regulate **commerce**, and declare war. For a law to pass, the House and Senate must both agree on the same version.

The legislative branch meets at the U.S. Capitol building.

Not-So-Popular Vote

The Constitution originally called for state **legislatures** to pick the Senate. A vote of the people chose members of the House. But the only people who could vote were those who were allowed to vote in state elections. In most states, that meant only free white men who owned property could vote.

Legislative Branch

(makes laws)

Congress

→ **Senate**
100 elected members total;
2 senators per state

→ **House of Representatives**
435 elected members total;
representatives based on each
state's population

Unfit for Office?

What if a bad leader gets into office? The Framers
gave Congress the power to remove officials—
even the president. The House can **impeach**
the president by accusing him of a crime.
The Senate then holds a trial to see if the
president should step down.

Enforcing the Laws

The Framers knew Congress would be useless if there was no way to enforce the laws it made. So, they created a new branch of government, which they called the executive branch. An elected president leads this branch.

Article II describes the executive branch. The president signs or **vetoes** laws made by Congress. He or she also enforces the laws, leads the armed forces, and makes **treaties**. The Framers feared having another king. So, they limited the president's powers. But, over time, the power of the presidency has grown.

Battle Tested

Article II says the president is **commander** in chief of the armed forces. Only one person has led troops in battle while he was president. That person was George Washington. In 1794, he led soldiers to stop a tax protest.

How to Pick a President

Some of the Framers thought Congress should pick the president. Others thought the public should vote. They came up with a compromise called the Electoral College. Each state gets a number of electoral votes that is based on its population. A candidate needs to get 270 electoral votes to become president.

Executive Branch

(carries out laws)

 President

President

 Vice President

Cabinet

Nominated by the president and must be approved by the Senate (with at least 51 votes)

The executive branch is based out of the White House.

Interpreting the Laws

Article III deals with the third branch of government, the judicial branch. The U.S. Supreme Court is in charge of this branch. The judicial branch has the power to interpret laws. But, the Framers were not clear on what this meant. Courts have used this power to reject some laws as **unconstitutional**.

Judicial Branch

(evaluates laws)

Supreme Court

9 justices nominated by the president; must be approved by the Senate (with at least 51 votes)

Other Federal Courts

No Escape

One part of Article VI was known as the **Fugitive** Slave Law. It said slave owners could go into free states to capture their enslaved people who had run away. Like the rest of the Constitution, this clause avoided using the word "slave."

Other Articles

Article IV says that states must respect the laws and court rulings of other states. Article V explains how to change the Constitution. Article VI confirms that the Constitution is the highest law of the land.

U.S. Supreme Court building

Treason Talk

Treason is the only crime that is defined in the Constitution. In England, charges of treason were used against people who said or wrote negative things about the government. The Framers tried to prevent that kind of abuse. They defined treason as waging war against the nation or helping its enemies.

Checks and Balances

The Framers did not want any branch of government to become too powerful. So, they came up with a system of checks and balances. Under this system, each of the three branches has ways to limit or block the actions of the other branches. Here are some of the most important checks and balances.

- Congress can reverse a veto by the president.
- Congress can remove the president through impeachment.
- Congress must approve the president's choices of U.S. Supreme Court justices and federal judges.
- Congress must approve cabinet members

Legislative Branch
(makes laws)

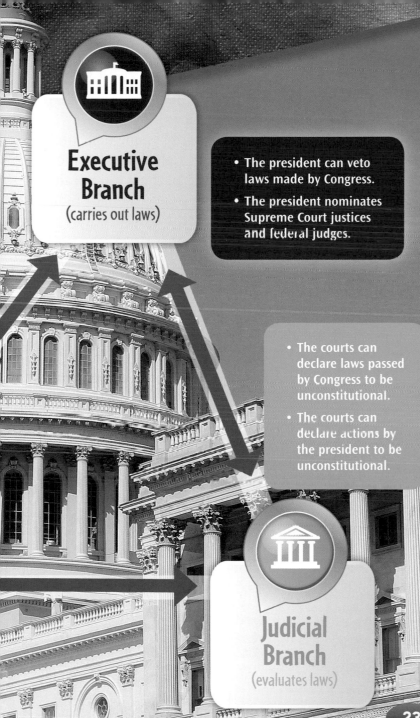

Executive Branch
(carries out laws)

- The president can veto laws made by Congress.
- The president nominates Supreme Court justices and federal judges.

- The courts can declare laws passed by Congress to be unconstitutional.
- The courts can declare actions by the president to be unconstitutional.

Judicial Branch
(evaluates laws)

The People's Rights

The Framers finally finished writing the Constitution in September of 1787. Some delegates wanted to add a list of people's rights. But the men had been meeting since May. Many of them did not think they needed to take extra time to add a bill of rights. In the end, 39 delegates signed the Constitution.

Next, it went to the states for their approval. Article VII said that nine states had to approve the Constitution for it to take effect. Leaders in some states wanted a list of people's rights. They agreed to ratify the Constitution only if a bill of rights would be added later. On June 21, 1788, New Hampshire became the ninth state to approve the document. The Constitution formally became the law of the land.

Jay's Journey

Before helping draft the Constitution, John Jay served as president of the Continental Congress. That was the group in charge of writing the Declaration of Independence. Jay also served as the country's first chief justice. That meant he was in charge of the U.S. Supreme Court.

Making the Case

Once the Framers had signed their names, the public debate began. Alexander Hamilton, James Madison, and John Jay wrote a series of newspaper articles. They told people how the new government would work. These articles are known as *The Federalist Papers*. People still study them to see what the Framers were thinking.

How to Amend the Constitution

After the states ratified the Constitution, the next step was to add the Bill of Rights. This could be done through the amendment process. Article V spells out this procedure for making changes to the Constitution. There are two ways to propose a new amendment. There are also two ways to ratify an amendment.

Propose a New Amendment

 Amendment is proposed by a two-thirds vote of each house of Congress.

 Amendment is proposed by a national convention called by Congress at the request of two-thirds of the state legislatures.

 Amendment is ratified by three-fourths of the state legislatures.

 Amendment is ratified by three-fourths of the state conventions.

Ratify a New Amendment

Bill of Rights

Madison was part of the new Congress that took office in 1789. He made a list of the rights all people should have. By 1791, the states ratified 10 of these rights, which became the first 10 amendments to the Constitution. They make up the Bill of Rights.

Free Expression

The First Amendment is about free expression. It protects freedom of religion, freedom of speech, and freedom of the press. It gives people the right to assemble—to gather and share ideas. And it protects the right to petition, or make a complaint, to the government.

Freedom of Faith

Many settlers came to the United States to escape being punished for their religions. But in some of the colonies, people were forced to be part of a certain church. The First Amendment says people can follow any faith. It says the government may not have an official church.

Martin Luther King Jr. (right) during the March on Washington in 1963.

Louder Than Words

Freedom of speech is not just for spoken words. It includes other forms of expression, such as protest marches and wearing armbands. But there are some exceptions. One rule says that people cannot say things that might cause harm to others. For example, it is illegal to yell, "fire!" in a crowded movie theater if there is no fire because people may panic and get hurt.

Because of Britain

Some amendments came as a direct result of the American Revolution. The British often arrested colonists without telling them why. The colonists could be kept in jail for a long time. The Bill of Rights aimed to stop these abuses.

The Fourth Amendment says police need good reasons to arrest or search people. The Fifth, Sixth, and Seventh Amendments spell out rules for trials. People accused of crimes have the right to quick trials by juries of their **peers**. The Eighth Amendment bans "cruel and unusual punishments." These rights still guide the justice system today.

Cruel and Unusual

While under British rule, people faced some nasty punishments for their crimes. Some people were marked with a letter that told of their crimes, such as a large "T" for a thief. For more serious crimes, people were beaten or had rocks thrown at them by people in the town. The Framers wrote the Eighth Amendment to protect people against such harsh punishments.

Unwelcome Guests

The British sometimes forced colonists to let soldiers stay in their homes. This was known as *quartering*. The Third Amendment says the government can't force people to quarter troops. Quartering is an issue that doesn't come up much in today's world, but it was a key issue when the Framers were writing the Constitution.

The war against Great Britain was fought in part by militias. The Second Amendment says a free country needs a "well regulated Militia." So, the amendment protects "the right of the people to keep and bear **Arms**."

People still argue about what these words mean. Some say the Framers meant that all people have a right to own guns. Others say the Framers only wanted to protect the right of militias to have guns.

The Ninth Amendment says people have rights beyond those in the Constitution. Courts have said this includes a right to privacy. The Tenth Amendment says that all of the rights that are not banned or given to the federal government are left to each state to decide.

An Army or a Militia?

Many of the Framers thought there should not be a full-time army when the country is not at war. They feared an army would make it hard for states to defend themselves against the federal government. That is why the Constitution allows Congress to approve money for an army, but only for two years at a time.

Bear Arms

The right to "keep and bear Arms" used to be in many countries' constitutions. In 1875, nearly one out of five constitutions around the world mentioned gun rights. But those numbers have fallen since then. Today, close to two hundred countries have constitutions. Of those, just three mention gun rights—Guatemala, Mexico, and the United States.

Rights for More Americans

The Framers settled many issues, but they failed on one key dispute. They did not resolve the nation's split over slavery.

That division led to the Civil War. During the war, President Abraham Lincoln **proclaimed** that enslaved people were now free. But he knew there must be a change to the Constitution. Then, in 1865, a man named John Wilkes Booth killed Lincoln. Eight months after his death, the country ratified the Thirteenth Amendment. It made slavery illegal.

Congress passed the Fourteenth Amendment in 1868. It was meant to help formerly enslaved people. It said all people were equal under the law. Two years later, the Fifteenth Amendment gave black men the right to vote.

Ending Slavery... Again

After the Civil War, many states in the South passed laws known as *black codes*. These were laws that forced newly freed people into unpaid labor. The laws made them live in a way that was similar to slavery. The laws served as a way to continue **oppressing** black people in the United States. The Fourteenth Amendment made these codes illegal.

slave auction, 1780

A Constitution for the South

The Civil War began when 11 Southern states broke away from the nation. These states wrote a new Confederate Constitution. A lot of it was the same as the U.S. Constitution, but there were key differences. The Confederate version used the word *slave*. It said slavery could not be outlawed.

Votes for Women

Women were encouraged when black men won their right to vote, because they wanted the same. But it would be 50 years before the Nineteenth Amendment gave women the right to vote.

Women played a major role in the war for independence and the fight to end slavery. But many men (and even some women) did not think women should vote. They said women should focus on their homes and children.

The struggle went on for decades. In 1917, women protested outside the White House for months. Finally, President Woodrow Wilson said he would support women. The Nineteenth Amendment was ratified in 1920. Women finally had the right to vote.

Old Enough to Vote

The rules were changed again in 1971 to let more people vote. The Twenty-Sixth Amendment lowered the voting age from 21 to 18. People who supported the change said that those who are old enough to go to war should be able to vote.

VOTE

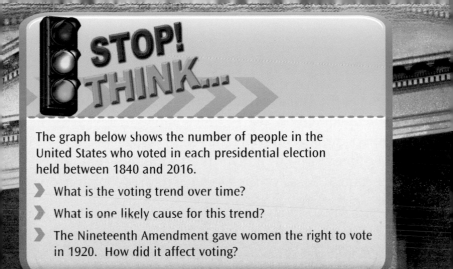

STOP! THINK...

The graph below shows the number of people in the United States who voted in each presidential election held between 1840 and 2016.

> What is the voting trend over time?

> What is one likely cause for this trend?

> The Nineteenth Amendment gave women the right to vote in 1920. How did it affect voting?

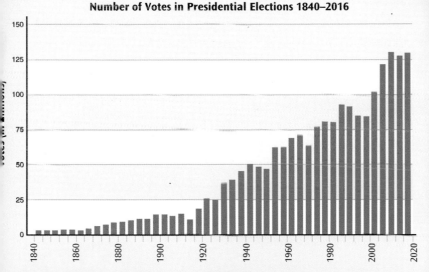

Number of Votes in Presidential Elections 1840–2016

Years

Changing with the Times

Since the Bill of Rights was added, the Constitution has been amended just 17 times in over 230 years. The Framers did a good job. They kept things broad to cover many situations. But they could not think of everything. Some of the changes to the Constitution came in response to big events.

For example, it does not say how many terms a president can serve. George Washington served two terms. Others followed his lead. But Franklin Roosevelt won a third term in 1940 and a fourth term in 1944. So Congress passed the Twenty-Second Amendment. It says the president can only serve two terms. The states ratified it in 1951.

Next in Line

Each time a president has died in office, the vice president has taken his place. But this process was not in the Constitution. When President John F. Kennedy was killed in 1963, leaders discussed the issue. Two years later, the country passed the Twenty-Fifth Amendment. It spells out what happens if a president dies or is unable to serve because of his or her health.

Dry Years

Only one amendment has been **repealed**. In 1919, the Eighteenth Amendment banned alcoholic drinks. This time was known as *Prohibition*. People got rich quick from the sale of illegal liquor. Crime rates rose. Leaders repealed the ban in 1933.

Two men pour alcohol into the sewers during Prohibition.

An Enduring Document

George Washington wrote that the Constitution was "little short of a miracle." He was amazed that the states had joined to form a new nation. At that time, the 13 states were home to almost 3 million people. Now, there are 50 states with more than 300 million people.

The Constitution has changed with the times. It has been amended at key points in the country's history. But the basic system has endured. Many people agree that what the Framers created truly was little short of a miracle.

The Constitutional vault, built in 1952, was built to lower 20 feet through the floor each night.

Glimpse of History

The original U.S. Constitution signed by the Framers is on display for the public. It is at the National Archives building in Washington, DC. The Declaration of Independence and the Bill of Rights are there, too. All three documents are kept in glass cases under low light to help protect them.

Glossary

amended—changed the wording or meaning of a law or document

arms—guns or other weapons

assuredly—without a doubt

commander—a person in charge of a group of people

commerce—activities related to buying and selling of goods and services

compromise—a way of reaching an agreement where everyone gives up something

congress—group of people who are in charge of making the laws for the country

convention—a large gathering of people who come together to make decisions

delegates—people chosen to speak for each of the colonies at a convention

electing—choosing a leader for a position by voting

endure—to continue to exist in the same way

federal—relating to the main government of the United States

Framers—the people who wrote the U.S. Constitution

fugitive—a person who runs away to keep from being captured

impeach—to charge a public official with a crime

interpret—to understand something in a particular way

legislatures—groups of people who have the authority to make laws

militia—regular citizens trained in military combat and willing to fight and defend their country

oppressing—treating a person or group of people in a cruel or unfair way

peers—people who belong to the same community as someone else

plantations—large farms that produce crops for money

Preamble—a statement at the beginning of the Constitution giving reasons for what follows

proclaimed—said in a public and official way

ratified—made official by signing or voting

repealed—thrown out, canceled

representatives—people who act or speak for others

treaties—formal agreements that are made between two or more countries or groups

unconstitutional—not allowed under the Constitution

unite—join together

vetoes—decides not to allow new laws to be passed

Index

Check It Out!

Books

Bradley, Kathleen. 2006. *The Constitution of the United States: Early America.* Teacher Created Materials.

Richmond, Ben. 2015. *What Are the Three Branches of the Government? And Other Questions About the U.S. Constitution.* Sterling Children's Books.

Videos

Liberty's Kids: Est. 1776. 2003. *We the People.* Public Broadcasting Service (PBS).

Websites

ConstitutionFacts.com. *What's Your Constitution IQ?* www.constitutionfacts.com

National Archives. *Meet the Framers of the Constitution.* www.archives.gov/founding-docs/founding-fathers

National Constitution Center. *Interactive Constitution.* www.constitutioncenter.org/interactive-constitution#

TeachingAmericanHistory.org. *Interactive Map of Historic Philadelphia in the Late 18th Century.* www.teachingamericanhistory.org/convention/map/

Try It!

Imagine you are a delegate at the Constitutional Convention. There are many important issues to discuss. Pick a key issue from that time period, and write a speech to deliver to your fellow delegates.

- There are many issues to choose from, such as slavery, representation, personal freedoms and rights, checks and balances, or presidential power.

- Research your topic, and gather facts to include in your speech.

- Clearly express your opinion on the issue in your speech. Make sure you include both facts and personal stories to support your reasoning.

About the Author

Margaret King grew up in San Diego County. She graduated from the University of California, Berkeley, with a degree in history and English. She also has a master's degree in journalism from Columbia University. King had different jobs at a newspaper. Later, she was a writer for Sally Ride Science, a company started by the first American woman in space. King and her husband live in San Diego. They have three grown children.